Tart Honey

Tart Honey

Deborah Burnham

RESOURCE *Publications* · Eugene, Oregon

TART HONEY

Resource Publications
An Imprint of Wipf and Stock Publishers
199 W. 8th Ave., Suite 3
Eugene, OR 97401

www.wipfandstock.com

PAPERBACK ISBN: 978-1-5326-4480-1
HARDCOVER ISBN: 978-1-5326-4481-8
EBOOK ISBN: 978-1-5326-4482-5

Manufactured in the U.S.A.

Contents

III.   Shadows Waver Between Your Shape and Mine

IV.   A shirt, a shroud

Some of these poems were included, many in different versions, in the chapbook *Still*, published by Seven Kitchens Press, winner of the Keystone Chapbook prize in 2008.

Unending thanks to David Staebler and Jeanne Walker.

I

The Rich Salt of Your Skin

M–Th

Because at Monday's dawn I kiss you hard
and won't touch your sweet mouth or hair again
until Friday's worked itself to shadow;

Because the years we've kissed add up to more
than those remaining to us, because
I want to squeeze time like an orange—

drinking the sweet juice, sweet flesh, eating
even the pith, the rind, wishing to find
another orange growing in the bitter seeds—

I've sent my dreams an order: no more
meandering through shadowed forests, no
casual lust for plums or single malt.

The new dream stays at home, to seize the time,
improve each shining dawn or midnight hour.
In Monday's dream, your hand sits on my thigh;

On Tuesdays, your cheek rests in my palm
like a willing apple; by Wednesday, our
feet are tangled, eager, and determined

to stay ensnared in one another. By
Friday, I'll have dreamed each limb and part
together, recalled the temperature and shape

of your absent body, making present what is far,
holding all that threatens to dissolve, disperse,
solid as the orange, distance's tart honey.

Modern Love

It's marriage *a la mode*, commuter
love; you leave with Monday's dawn and stay
away while four more dawns unfold across
my single sheets. You left your worn gray
shirt. I'll fold it in my pillow and write
a letter with my breath, one word over
and again: your name, mouthed into the shirt's
soft threads where the rich salt of your skin still clings.

Eking Out

I watched *Apollo 13* with you, marveling
at the ground crew's loving calculations:
how much air and power they had per day,
per hour, after the broken ship exhaled
a shimmering cloud of oxygen into space,
which does not need to breathe.

Such useful lessons. How to use them now?
On Friday nights, you're home, I have you
for two days, three nights, just sixty hours
to divide among my hands, my lips, back, belly,
trembling arms, each part ravenous, snatching
its full share.

One More

Catullus, wondering how to count the kisses
that would satisfy his lust for Lesbia,
suggests a number: the grains of sand between
Jove's oracle in Egypt and some tomb
in Libya, or—less original—the numbered fields
of stars that try to light their furtive love.

We've loved so long, I forget what "furtive"
feels like, though years ago, we could kiss only
in dark rooms, dark fields, hiding the thin fire that leapt
through our legs and fingers.

Now, it's one brisk, public kiss that makes me think
of those I won't be tasting for a week or three,
that short kiss in airport traffic, stolen
while the cop stares, one brush against
your earlobe, then one more, quicker, drier
than our first, perhaps our last, this last thought
unthinkable, the necessary single
star that glitters, once so far away, now
right above us, behind the waning moon.

Some Days

When you're away, I cannot count
my fingers, clumped into a fist.
Days slide like pennies in a drawer.

I'm like the man who fell
headfirst on the stony path
and lost his numbers. Couldn't count

the days to Friday or add
the nickels in his pocket. Seconds
blurred and minutes wouldn't pass.

When you come back, I count
grapes and sips of wine. Each minute
says its name too clearly, each day
steps away, *one two*, *one* two,
and then it's gone.

Blue Nudes

1. The Dyer's Hands

> Matisse prepared huge sheets of paper
> for his cutouts, painting them the solid
> blue of crayons, of his water jug, then sliced
> in with his ten-inch shears. His hands, stained blue,
> shaped dancing bodies, caressed the thick blue
> paper into long slow ovals,
>
> making our bodies think that his idea
> of a body was the first one, and the best.
> His dancers move like greyhounds, like blue
> flutes that bend into their low notes, then curve
> out again; we stretch our hands into the moonlight,
> hoping to see blue.

2. Our Hands

> My hands, your hands, assume the color
> of each other's bodies in the streetlight's
> acrid gold. At dawn, our skins are simplified
> to blue, so pure, so softly curved you'd think
> that we could stretch into the dancer's lean
> blue shapes, love softening our querulous
> aging flesh. You stroke my back where I cannot
> reach, so gently I wonder if the touch
> is yours, or the pure blue light.

Peaches

1.

Peaches on a blue plate, on blue linen,
ripening as slowly as the sun
fades into night. Sometimes wind will make them
fall so softly that they lie unbruised
among the rough grass, the knobby roots.
I'd like to cut ripe peaches for you,
lay one bright crescent, then another
on your tongue so you could squeeze the juice
around your mouth, then kiss me.

2.

The sage who counseled "Live in the exact
center of each moment" must have had one
ripe peach in mind, in hand, his mouth
dry from trying to say "no" so gently
to Desire, in late August when the lightest
touch on rosemary or basil sends sharp
perfume into the air like smoke, so willing
to diffuse itself into the dry heat.

On waking every hour

Trickster moonlight spreads like ice
across the leaves, leaving my
bewildered skin to wonder how
to sleep when the moon swells

to a ball of ice, then melts,
pouring light that behaves like water
on piping birds, vines knotted at
our window, and your exhausted arms.

Leaves, skin, and the fields beyond us
dip and coil in the moon's glaze that
settles, thick as the iced river, on our bed.
We shift and whisper into sleep;

I count your breaths while the wet moon
spills itself on sleeping birds,
startling them into song before my
shadow unfolds on the loose air of dawn.

On the gift of a photograph

Thank you for the picture of November roses,
unmarked by frost. Thanks for telling me
about Andre Kertesz, and how in 1915
he snapped two Polish soldiers on their field latrine,
and how he kept their dignity clean and useful
like the straw they clutched.

One story says that Kertesz sent the photo
to one soldier's widow. Not likely—but if he did,
I bet she thanked him for believing that a man's
last printed moment is worth keeping,
even if his pants are down.

I've stopped editing the awkward moments from our
life-film—our yawns, snores, belches, silences, leaving
them intact beside our loving grins, like November
roses shocking pink against a filthy sky,
their petals curled and ruffled, as artful as the straw
braid one soldier plaited, glossy as a girl's, lovely
against their scars.

The night the screen fell out

a gray bat whispered through our room, though "whisper"
is too loud a word for how it swooped and dipped,
barely wrinkling the smooth air.

Because my mother shows me what it is
to live bravely with no other body
in the house; because one night she woke

to find a bat sitting in her hair,
then gently shook it from her fingers,
and did not cry, or let it fly into her dream,

I knew that solitary air can be disturbed,
then quickly sleep again, that loneliness
can soften into solitude. Some days

your absence hovers silently, the bat
at play around my head, more like a thought
of sound than sound itself.

Loose

To remember how your shoulders weigh against my chest
I must think of things that are nothing like a breathing body;

I must recall the night I nearly drowned, the weight of water
beating on me from all sides. I did not swallow

what the lake was offering; I felt the water's grip unclenching,
and for a minute did not recognize my skin, uncertain, loosened;

the way, without you, my skin forgets its proper boundaries
and for a moment, before sleep, I am water spilling into sand.

Cornbread

Tonight I'll eat alone because, in the tug
of war between Liebe and Arbeit, work
has pulled you north, me south, so I'm sulking
on my solitary couch, eating cornbread
doused with milk,

remembering the widower next door who ate
milk and cornbread every night, finding what would
suffice, though I'm sure he never said "suffice."
Aztecs called themselves the golden people
of the corn,

because the kernels, plump with their sweet
milk, made them like gods, hot-yellow as the sun,
stretching to the milk-white sky. So, I heap
my sky-blue bowl with god-food to fill
my heart and gut.

The widower spent forty years learning
what's enough, compared with what he had,
and, "praise be," he said, they were the same.
The paper-hatted quart, the ten-cent box

of Jiffy Cornbread mix, good for a day
or more, pale yellow sun, enough to sustain a god
even when he's alone and hungry.

Here, There

1.

When you're gone, I watch Love smiling
at itself: kisses on the bus,
loud embraces in the train,fat ochre fish in the stream
of gratified desire. I'm
the cormorant, your absence
a tight ring around my neck,
no room to swallow fish of any
size, or water, just the empty air.

2.

When you're away, I sleep on your side
of our old bed. Perhaps that side will sink
like the stretch of meadow where an old
horse naps on a damp afternoon,
lowering its heavy bones to the shallow
bowl, where the tough grass bends.

3.

When you come back, the moon
cracks like a silver melon
dropped on granite.
We are two moons hanging in the dark,
circling the cadmium of melon-fire,
the sunset's peach and ochre,
a light that will return.

When you have been away too long,
I think about Penelope

Let's say she told the suitors she believed Odysseus
was dead. Let's say she claimed a dream told her to weave
a mourning shawl from his long hair, but since, she said,
it wafts like seaweed in the unforgiving ocean,
she would need hair from another honored head.

I think they'd have run at her like hungry dogs, pulling
hanks of hair and piling them around her. And she'd be
happy; it would take her days to comb and spin
that hair, to prepare the loom, so she'd let them grease
their chins with her husband's roasted cows,

mix their rough wine while she wove the shawl,
a charm against the dogs of loneliness.
When her dreams said "he's coming back," she'd soak
the shawl in oil, hold it near the torch,
and throw it into their huddle as they slept.

II

We'd Wake Early and Eat Apples

Erasures: Bonnard

1.

Afraid to say "I love you," I'd breathe,
erasing my bold wish and say instead
"I love snow" or ". . . swimming."
Any word, erased, leaves marks;
no desire half-spoken vanishes forever.

2.

Bonnard would lay a swatch of blue, wonder
what blue demands in April light, then add
a wash of yellow to make it more purely
blue. Even with the painting sold, he'd wonder
if the plum's cheek was shadowed, so he'd slide
into the gallery, a tiny paint box
in his pocket, and correct its ruddiness, its streaks.

3.

I long to keep you with me, and to speak
that longing when sunlight marks a stone.
Bright patches fade and darken,
like the shadows Bonnard changed in his last
painting. His nephew helped him paint the soil
near a flowering almond tree from green
to gold. "You can't have too much yellow."

She invented the cup

by bending toward a stream, hands curving
in an open shape that no one called
a cup, yet, bringing cold green water
to her lips, sucking it like air,
like our first kiss, secret, gulping. Soon
she saw cups waiting: clamshells, the halved
skulls of deershe could pour clean water
on her infant's sweaty head and watch it
pooling in his fontanel. She'd kiss him
there, a tiny sip of water warmed
by his bones and hair

                          the way we kissed
at first, my arched throat, your curving palms,
hollows holding air and salt for us to drink.

Two Aprils

April spills unruly light across
your sleeping cheek. I'm half-awake, reading
someone's elegy for his wife, keeping
his grief at arm's length, slipping my free hand
into your shirt to find your skin's sweet salt.

My eyes blur: it's 1969, spring,
we're watching *Let It Be*, acrid smoke filling
our hair, the bloody summer not yet here,
the war immune to prayer or fire. We eat
samosas with our hands, a bit high, drowsy,
we stroke each other's hands, the slick sweet oil.

You turn; my book falls against my sleeping face.
I'm dreaming things that didn't happen,
I didn't know you then, years until we'd kiss,
but I invent a history for us: more time to cherish,
more to lose, more time to feed you bread
and honey with my bare hands, while you lick
the oozing drops.

Winter Apples

Long ago, we'd wake at dawn,
eat apples, hard, acid-green,
twirled knives through spots, brown pulp
sweet as earth after soft rain,
or so I thought wet earth
might taste. Love was so new
I had to learn it day by day,
learn how your sweet skin could taste
like bread, or the salty pebbles
that flecked the sand.

When September pulled you west,
I'd buy pounds of apples, yellow,
green, and pile them in glass bowls,
green mellowing to gold,
because the Romans said ripe
fruit was honored best by glass.
I'd cut one, saving the hardest,
greenest against your coming.

I still buy too many apples
because you leave at dawn
to drive miles of apple-roads.
My mouth, sweet from the warm
salt of your cheek, wants apple—
remembering dry summers
when we ate our stubborn fruit,
tasting snow in the sharp green
skin, cider swelling under the light bruise.

Ripen, or Not

Once, we ran three miles in August heat, then lay,
flushed and grimy, on the bare floor while a storm
raced off the lake. Wet wind rinsed the dusty
willows, flowed across our stiff and filthy
skins. Rain through the curtains drenched the bowl
of hard green pears, the red plums I'd kept
cold and sour, as if by forbidding them
to ripen I could stop time and keep you here.

Baseball

I love your hands when we talk baseball, how
they move like the thoughtful jazz that holds us
close to sleep. Like jazz, baseball rushes,
pauses to think about itself, then takes off again.
We laugh sometimes, like John Donne grinning

at his lover, their eyebeams twisted
to a double string, so connected they could see
inside each other's thoughts, like the pitcher
and his catcher trading signals, like the pianist
and bass who feel each other's syncopated

heartbeats. Art Tatum was too blind to see
his partners, or his fingers as they struck
a thousand notes a minute, sound cascading
into incandescence.
      He'd hear the Tigers
on the radio, then recite the play-

by-play while driving home at 3 a.m.
after four long sets, arpeggios still rippling
through his ears
        and yes, you tell me,
he was driving, that blind genius cruising
a huge Buick through the empty streets, talking

baseball to the friend beside him, three hands
gently on the wheel, the game unfolding slowly

the way you slowly tell me how your hands
and tongue are eager, waiting, like a simple
four-bar tune that warms up into light
and speed, then lies back, waiting.

Counting

Someone claimed you can't count silence
but surely there's a number for the silence

of a field of apple trees, April blossoms
dried by frost, blowing like dirty snow;

for the silence of the nets, tangled near the lake
that swarms with fish who are all bone, grinning;

for the silence of the bells whose heavy tongues have
fallen to the rock and cannot move,

bells that once invited us to fill ourselves
with bread and hope, and water that was as good

as hope, and better because it filled our cups and pitchers
splashing, rippling, breaking the dry silence
of all our absences.

The House

Some days, the house contains me
as a seashell cups its creature,
soft as an infant's palm
inside its pearly spiral,
no rough skin protecting it.

Days ripple through like warm seas
flowing through the shell and out again,
rinsing places where my body never moves.

Some days are September evenings, old sun in the gingko
turning white plates, bleached cloths, to gold and amber,
just light enough to read a page.

2.

Some days, I set the table as if I planned
to paint the cloth, the terracotta bowl
of apricots, the green vase of nodding
lilies. Some days move so quietly,
so slowly that the lilies' fragile dusty
horns are barely drooping in the late sun.
The infantine skin of apricot grows soft
but does not fade or wrinkle.

What it was like

Once, days were always gray, a dozen winters
rasping on bare wood,

shade of the half-remembered, substance without
frame or spine,

the hesitation before speech. My silence had forgotten
what to say, and why,

my voice a rasp of hesitation on a granite step.
I tasted dust, saw dust

across your body, as if seeing you blurred and far away
was all I'd get.

III

Shadows Waver Between
Your Shape and Mine

With This Ring

1. Short Procedures Room

   She listens to the nurse: they cut her husband's
   wedding ring to save his finger. She holds
   a Baggie: the ring glows, the cut piece
   rattles in the corner.

   I say "It can be fixed" and she says "Sixty
   years" and I show my ring that once glowed
   on my grandmother's knobbed hand, where it said
   "widow" twice as long as "wife."

2. Single Ring Ceremony

   You didn't want a ring—just a symbol,
   we agreed—and our life was going to be
   one built on substance. Now I lock the door
   behind you every week, my ring a narrow
   circle where I walk and sleep, room enough
   for one.

Quoting Sappho

Catullus tells us how he gawked across the table
while the one he wanted chatted with her lover,
who might have dipped a chunk of bread in oil
then held it, dripping, against her lips.

Catullus tells us how his sinews loosened,
how he remembered words he'd learned from Sappho,
the thin, or soft, or gentle fire streaming
through his muscles. His breath halts, thrums—

So I think: *poor Catullus*, as I sit without you,
miles of highway as my rival. Just thinking
of your angled profile, your thinking hands,
I feel my cold flesh softening

and I warm myself, make my breath stop or leap,
remembering that sweet Sappho knew exactly
how the tongue fails, flailing across words like *fire*
and *rush*, sitting close to one she loved,
far from saying what she meant or wanted.

Second Skin

You're far away; I'm here, my wife-skin slack
across my shoulders, wondering how to live
without its binding strength.

There's a story of a wife who dropped her skin,
wrinkling, on the floor, then left to fish, or sing,
far from her family's wail and grime,
then came back, stepped into that skin and fixed
their breakfast.
                    Another ending says she wrapped
the skin around her naked flesh, then screamed—
her husband salted it to make her wonder
why she'd left—while she writhed against the burn
she couldn't rinse away.

I've made the skin into a robe, a garment
falling softly from my shoulders. It ripples
in the breeze of your return; its shadow
wavering between your shape and mine.

Dry

August: leaves browning at the edge,
while the ground cracks, and blossoms crackle;

air sags, soaked and heavy, so full of water
you'd think it could collect itself and fall

as pure rain, coaxing green into the sere
and battered leaves.

In Chile, where sand stays parched for months,
they hang huge fine-meshed nets near the seaside

so when the seawind blows dense fog ashore,
it dangles on the nets like wet pearls, then falls

in a silvery clear stream to waiting
barrels to be poured on corn and beans

and a child's dry cup.
                              And on humid
mornings, I move dry fingers through the air

wishing I could gather water because
after days of absence, just a word,

a touch would wake me as the rain wakes
dry roots coiled in sand.

Peach Trees

1.

In spring, the limbs are wrapped in blossoms,
which even literal eyes must see as snow,
unless you look at snow and see an April
orchard from horizon to horizon.

2.

The dying tree is full of peaches, dried
to the size of blue plums, but wrinkled
orange like the hard, deep, desert sunset.

3.

Fragile, warmed by August, these ripe fruits
are like a baby's skull; we haven't held
a child for twenty years and grow clumsy
with these furred globes in our palms, wondering
if we've lost the tenderness that seemed so easy.

Bite

My rough capped tooth slices at
my tongue's soft reluctant meat each time
I speak, so I've been holding back from daily
speech, pointing, grimacing, saving my few
words for fine distinctions

and apologies. You kiss me, slow,
deep; your tongue grazes that small blade
and you pull back, startled, at the sharp rebuke
delivered without warning. We never
knew my body would try hurting you,
so deep, so sudden.

Fever

You're far away, in Santa
Clara, Fe, or Barbara:
I'm sick, too wobbly to pour
an icy glass; my hot ears hum

the words to "Fever." It lasts *all
through the night* and even night's
cool hand can't ease it. Fever

locks its arms around me,
not the love-sweat we could share
if you were close and whispering.

Now nothing's close but fever, taunting
What if he won't come back?
I'm a sick child frightened
in a fever dream, knowing
it's not true, but what if, what if.

Heat Exchange: Abishag

> Now King David was old, and his servants said,
> let there be sought a young virgin, let her lie in
> thy bosom so that the lord the king may get heat.
>
> First Kings 1

When the King dies, she will be sent home, used
and useless, thinking that a man's ribs
are cold stone rods against her cheek. His skin
is a dry field where the flesh of men
and horses crushed the grass. His hands repeat
a battle on her back, but he has lost
the joy that bubbled in his groin;
he sang while thrusting swords that now
he cannot lift. He tries to sing to her; his breath
is warm, like the faint heat in folds of air
where his stories lie.

Maybe Abishag held shawls against her
chest to swaddle the chilled king. When a shawl
grew cool, she'd bring another. She was young
and never cold, and did not wonder,

as I do, how many winters you will offer
your flushed shoulders to my blue hands,
how long my forehead will take slow heat
from your cheeks, palms, and lips.

Waking

Most nights, it's the lonely backyard celibate
cat that wails me out of sleep while the proud
clock displays the difference between 3:00
and 3:01, a finger-width of time
smaller than the blank place in the bed.

When you're here, you wake twice, three times each night;
I wake with you; we listen for the cat,
screeching against empty spaces, yowling
against the early dark, and we say "yes" and "thanks"
and reach across each other's shoulders and hold on.

Word into Flesh

When our words are all I have of you,
the last words from each night's call,
years of "sleep well" and "love,"

surely those words, so long repeated
take on some weight, some heft
heavier than the air that carries them.

Like cold mist, insubstantial,
they're collecting on the window,
condensing to bright drops that roll

and spill into a pool, then freeze
into a solid round, a shape that takes
up space, thick enough to cast a shadow.

What if our late-night words could thicken
into flesh and sinew? If I looked
closely, I could make out your shape—

cropped head, rough stubble.
I reach toward you; something
whispers *Do not touch,*
I am not here.

Dry Day Blues

Woke up this morning to the catbird's single cry:
no brazen imitations of the fluting
robin, the gate-latch squeak of squirrel, just a thirsty
one-note rasp as if she's clearing her hot throat.

Woke this dry day mouthing a single word.
When you're far away, our nightly phone calls
shrink like the drying leaves our sycamore
throws down, the edges crackling dead and brown.

Woke up this morning tasting dry leaves, dust across
my tongue, waiting for dusk and the dry buzz
of the phone, practicing my one word: _hold_
perhaps, or _when_. Woke this morning thirsty,

searching my mouth for water, my tongue
like paper, but too rough to write my scrawled
song, its single burden _home is here come_ home.

Translation

When I ask you for salt

> I'm asking you to kiss my hair,
> thick and sweaty as I run along the lake, alone

When I pour your water

> I'm asking you to talk to me
> until your tongue grows dry and thin

If I asked you to play a wooden flute

> I'd just want to hear you breathing.

If I asked you to make bread from dust,

> I'd be saying, *Stay. Just* stay.

Water

contains all colors, though
each cancels out its opposite.

Green makes red invisible;
lavender silences sharp yellow.

Nothing left but gray, the winter
lake that freezes color in its bed,

except a bit that thaws and flows
into my lonely sleep: your eyes'
warm inky blue.

IV

A Shirt, a Shroud

Since we can still call each other "love"

I'm asking you to watch the knife-edge
of dawn over the slow river

sky slit by rose or gray as it has been
each day, enough like the day before

though some day will be the last
this knowledge hovering like a hand

the touch exploring the cool margins
of a time we will not have, the touch

that takes me to the comfortable
half-beat of time propped on the edge

of sleep, that moment when I feel
a hand, light on my chest, and wonder
if it is mine or yours

Parts and Wholes

1.

When she was little, we'd do jigsaws, guessing
what the pieces were, sometimes saying "flower"
for a clown-face, but soon she understood:
each piece had its locked-in place.
I'd put her firmly in her bed, held in
by monkey, bear, and doll, each object
in its place, limbs, paws, and tails curving
softly around each other.

2.

Old couples stay together touching edges,
pieces wearing down, but only as their
counterparts are worn, still fitting gently
next to one another, soft and blurred,
but practiced, sure.

The Body of the Water

Each wave was long, a muscle rising
on the back of some thoughtful animal,
one I'd like to stroke but dared not
breach the shadow of his awful strength.

Each wave spread its smooth strong tube across
the sand, then opened like a scroll with secrets
inked on the hidden page—perhaps the moment
that we'll touch each other for the last time—

then splitting, thick foam unraveling across
its sudden length, a steady white against
the blue that pales from cobalt to thin aqua
then darkens as another wave arises,

unrolls so high it casts a shadow back
behind itself. I know it shades the cobalt
almost purple; I know your every touch
can change my flesh, warm, calm, as waters
alter, magnify each other.

Useful

(after Catullus, Poem 7)

The snarky Roman cites the ancient practice of tossing
old men from bridges when they'd reached sixty,
"the age of uselessness."

Even daft and crippled, old women were of use. Families
kept them to peel onions and hem shirts. Our County Home
housed ninety men, two women.

I'm thinking about "useful" because you, my love, turn sixty
in the spring. You leave sweet traces of your breath, your hair-
sweat on the pillow which I fold

against my cheek the nights you're gone, when rough air
whistles through the latched glass fast enough to scatter
those wispy scents

sweet as wet earth around a hoe, the hollow damp clinging
to an oar, moving water from the crumbling bank
to the moss-hung piles

that hold a bridge we'll cross someday, if not hand in hand,
perhaps just a few steps separating my last breath from your last
word, or otherwise.

Ars Poetica: Linen

My last poems will be tough, like linen.

The sailor's linen trousers held a year of salt and oil.
When the Pharaoh's tomb was opened, the linen
curtains hung intact.

Those poems will walk in a single line like the linen
thread that marked a furrow for the oxen,
plowing sodden fields.

They will be useful; they will make the heavy bag
that holds the rising bread, gives shape to the eager
yeast, taming it to a loaf.

And though Leviticus forbids the garment of mixed threads,
my mothers wove wool and linen into warm enduring
fabric, the useful linsey-woolsey.

Poems should be warm; they should bend around
the body of my love, a blanket that might be hung for curtains,
a shirt long and wide enough to shroud two bodies, all at once.

Where

If I ever find my golden earring
in the dull shoals of paper on the floor;
if I see it glinting, like a lost coin
on a rocky shore, tempting gulls
who love bright things,

I'll stitch the earring in your shoe,
a charm against some greater loss
in case you need to buy safe passage
across whatever river lies between your body
in the blazing car or crumpled airplane
and some land beyond.

Two rings might purchase you a moment here.
I've heard that sea-gods give a drowned man
one last look at the dry world and its wrack
of objects, one glimmering visit
to his love's bed to wake her, to say he's gone, goodbye.

Will

The man I've loved for forty years will die
in less than forty years and, like most men,
he has not willed his precious objects.

The tiny boat my father scraped and polished
like a tea chest sits, slowly cracking.
My dead friend's cello dries in its velvet bed.

The man I love has bought a table, cut
and polished like the cello's back, sleek
as a keel. When he no longer sits there,

I will soak and bend it to a boat,
and take my grief to sea, an inch of wood
between my skin and the abrading
salty sun.

New Widow

Because women in my mother's family
live more years as widows than as wives,
they could write a manual for the first years
of grief, which come without directions.

You must do everything yourself, at once.
You must pay for all the air moving through
the house, though there's only one of you
still breathing.

You must unfold the crumpled air to loose
the tunes he murmured. Let them float
into the wavering curtains to dissolve
like dust in rain.

You must fix the tap where a cold string
of water hangs. It tastes like him—
his hands and hair.

Grief

thirsty even as I drain the glass
my tongue so dry it scrapes my cheek
which is also dry

tongue and cheek two sheets of paper rasping
against each other, the small
resistant pain

each page with verses from a language
whose syntax cannot walk with mine
without a limp

words translated into watered wine,
a song heard through rain

2.

seeking a single word

for what we strain to say in tangled phrases
in Korean, *bosulbii* means one thing: a thin
rain on a windless day

people who live in snow have words
for flakes that fall like gravel, another for those
that softly lose their shape against your cheek

and will I someday find the word for the breath between
despair and the whisper
perhaps it can be borne

though silent, still, uncaring

Aubade on King Richard's Bones

My morning song's directed to the sun:
slow down, let darkness blanket us until
we're weary of each other's skin, tumbled
in our clean bed, our S-curves sliding
into one another. The room's still dark,

but not as dark as Richard's grave where his
bones lay, six hundred years, compacted under
clay and tar, spine in the S-curve he was
born with, Nature's error, Nurture's victory.
He lived with what he had not, as we do,

living with absence, distance, a skewed normal.
Widowed Richard had no one to beg
the sun slow down, no one to keep him lying
half asleep on his last morning, no one
to pray for hail and rain, ruining the field,

to keep his skull safe from blade and arrow.
Richard rose that day with work to do;
he could not linger, floating on his martial
linen, probably stained dust-gray. He rose;
spiked sun might have bored into his eyes.

Perhaps he blinked, saw a field of white:
bleached sheets, pale roses, anything but
the flash of steel; blinked as I do, out of sleep
into *now, farewell,* my dawn song, praising
the sky that flares to white, dawn that comes
with its bright burden whether I sing or not.

If ever I would leave you

I'd have to leave you from a single room where I'd set
a bowl of apples drying on the sill, where I'd torn
blue letters, pieces smaller than my moments
of regret, and scattered them like dry leaves that whisper
as you walk.

I'd have to stand alone and chill in a tall gray
station, trains filling the air with steam, travellers who speak
their darkening farewells in words that fall against my ears
like rough birdsong.

If I left you, I'd have to wait for days while trains filled
with crowds of damp gray coats. If you came searching, my dress
would turn gray, I'd be invisible, holding nothing
but a parcel

wrapped in twine, strand winding around strand, protecting
what's inside—the hollow, foreign air that chills a kiss,
our choked farewells.

Returning

I think our dead come back to taste one fragrant
strawberry, or sip of rough black
coffee. They must like standing in the odor
of warm bread, the dish of honey. So it's right
to offer up the infant's nape, the line-dried
sheet, the peppercorn just cracked to any
of our dead who might be waiting.

I'll come to you in a flash of starched
white sleeve, or cotton sheet rising
and sinking in the sunset breeze. Or,
in the stubborn oil of rosemary, the herb
of memory, that once touched will scent
your hand all day.

Revenant

If you came back to me
not as a warm word, a sweet breath,
but a pile of bone,

would I be afraid to lift
your skull up to the hard sun
to see what's left:

letters written on the smooth walls—
your last words, or our first word
of timid love—

or might it be filled with spiky
jewels that flare in sunlight but
spell nothing?

To practice loss

is easier these days as last breaths
accumulate like the hard dry leaves

that, spiraling down, open a hands-width
of November sky. Perhaps one day

in ten it shines like the deep steel
gray-blue of your eyes, which no practice,

however long or dutiful,
could teach me how to lose.

Grief and Water

1.

What if our griefs grew loose
and clear as water?
Impossible to live
on water, only;
impossible to live without.

2.

Like water, grief encloses you
in a loose embrace that marks
your clothes and skin. Look, here's
my mourning dress: black silk,
with watermarks from hem to bodice,
like lines on old maps, undulating,
connecting one grief to another
so you never have to leave the path.

One way to end

There are a thousand stories of old people,
speechless, confused, who wander to the woods
and disappear behind a screen of briar.
They are so light, so frail, they barely leave
a footstep through the soft duff of leaf
and needle, like the old scouts whose
moccasins left no print.

I might leave the house to look for you, walking
a straight line, turning only to avoid
a sapling, a fallen log, but as the woods
thicken, I'll leave bits of clothing—a sleeve,
a shoe, caught on the encircling limbs.
I'll walk so near the great rough trunks that,
cell by cell, my grateful drying flesh
will wear to nothing against the dry sound
of crumpling leaves, so worn their traceries
of vein can't cast a shadow.

I've loved you as I've loved the sun

waiting through its changing lights:
jets of flame across the west
that fade gray like a shirt
that won't bleach back to white,

then a run of days with all
the blues our eyes have ever seen,
in the lake, around a cloud, deep
in the forget-me-not.

You've warmed me every morning
all our lives, your hands tight on my stiff
shoulders. My mouth warms yours in our
inevitable, faithful, quick goodbye.

Now I must learn to love you as
I love the moon, so rarely here
in full round glow, but always
somewhere, hidden, or half-visible,

regular in its increase, practiced
decline and vanishing. I've learned
to cherish the faint, sharp curve
of light, the bold half, cut like

a melon, the swollen creamy
dish at full, two nights or three, then
out of darkness, the thin pearl
scimitar again, cupping a month of light.

One hundred words for snow

The flake the grain the frozen dot
sodden, silent, dry, and clicking
against glass, cutting eyelids .

Each snow-word, sifting to the ground,
caresses others, piling softly
as a blanket, freezing to the touch,

but capable of sheltering the naked
ground, thin branches, from the killing
wind so they'll turn green in April.

All the words I have for loving
you come down to six or so:
take this kiss   here   my hand

repeated, whispered, laughed. These words,
so small, so light, accumulate
like snow—a blanket, airy, clean,

that tastes of cold, that covers us
and warms us, lets us sink into
a long sleep where warm and cold,

here and there, dissolve into
a single word that we can speak all night.

www.ingramcontent.com/pod-product-compliance
Lightning Source LLC
Chambersburg PA
CBHW060158070426
42447CB00033B/2208